Haircuts

Level 4 – Blue

Helpful Hints for Reading at Home

The graphemes (written letters) and phonemes (units of sound) used throughout this series are aligned with Letters and Sounds. This offers a consistent approach to learning, whether reading at home or in the classroom.

HERE IS A LIST OF PHONEMES FOR THIS PHASE OF LEARNING. AN EXAMPLE OF THE PRONUNCIATION CAN BE FOUND IN BRACKETS.

Phase 3			
j (jug)	v (van)	w (wet)	x (fox)
y (yellow)	z (zoo)	zz (buzz)	qu (quick)
ch (chip)	sh (shop)	th (thin/then)	ng (ring)
ai (rain)	ee (feet)	igh (night)	oa (boat)
oo (boot/look)	ar (farm)	or (for)	ur (hurt)
ow (cow)	oi (coin)	ear (dear)	air (fair)
ure (sure)	er (corner)		

HERE ARE SOME WORDS WHICH YOUR CHILD MAY FIND TRICKY.

Phase 3 Tricky Words			
he	you	she	they
we	all	me	are
be	my	was	her

Phase 4 Tricky Words			
said	were	have	there
like	little	so	one
do	when	some	out
come	what		

TOP TIPS FOR HELPING YOUR CHILD TO READ:

- Allow children time to break down unfamiliar words into units of sound and then encourage children to string these sounds together to create the word.

- Encourage your child to point out any focus phonics when they are used.

- Read through the book more than once to grow confidence.

- Ask simple questions about the text to assess understanding.

- Encourage children to use illustrations as prompts.

This book focuses on /ear/ and /air/ and is a Blue level 4 book band.

Can you sort all the words on this page into two groups?

Gear

Year

Words with **ear**

Pair

Chair   Stairs

Words with **air**

Tear

Hear

What happens when you get a haircut?

You sit in a chair to get a haircut. This chair is big and black.

A cloak will catch the hair that is cut off.

Snip, snip. The hair is cut near the top.

The clippers buzz near his ear. They trim the hair to the right length.

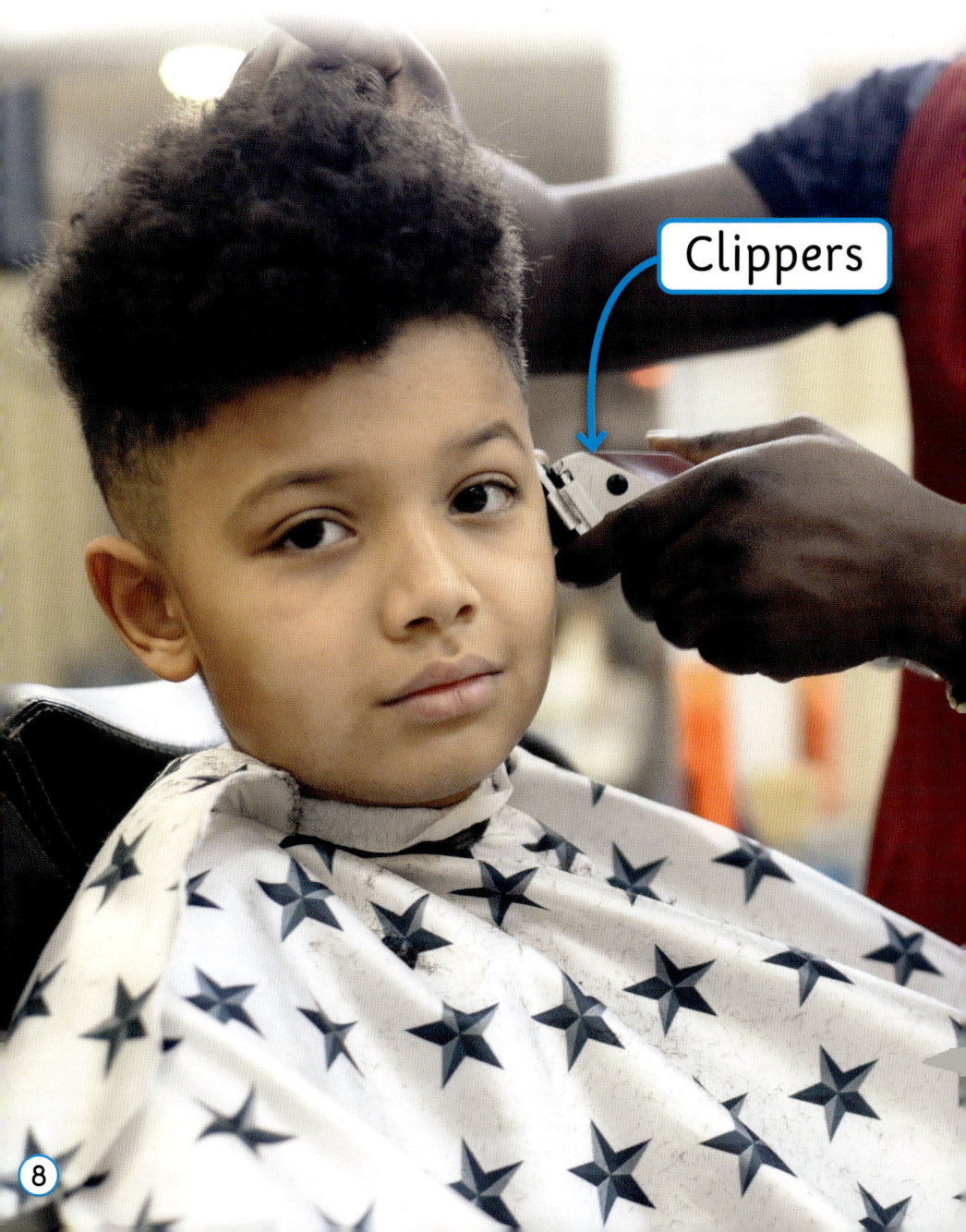

Clippers

Her hair is long. She needs a trim. She will get a little bit cut off near her back.

They might need to pin long hair up with a clip to cut it.

Clip

They gather up a lock of hair and cut it near the end.

Beards can be cut and trimmed. The man will need to sit still.

They trim it near his neck and near his ear.

They trim some beard hair near his lip. It is neat now.

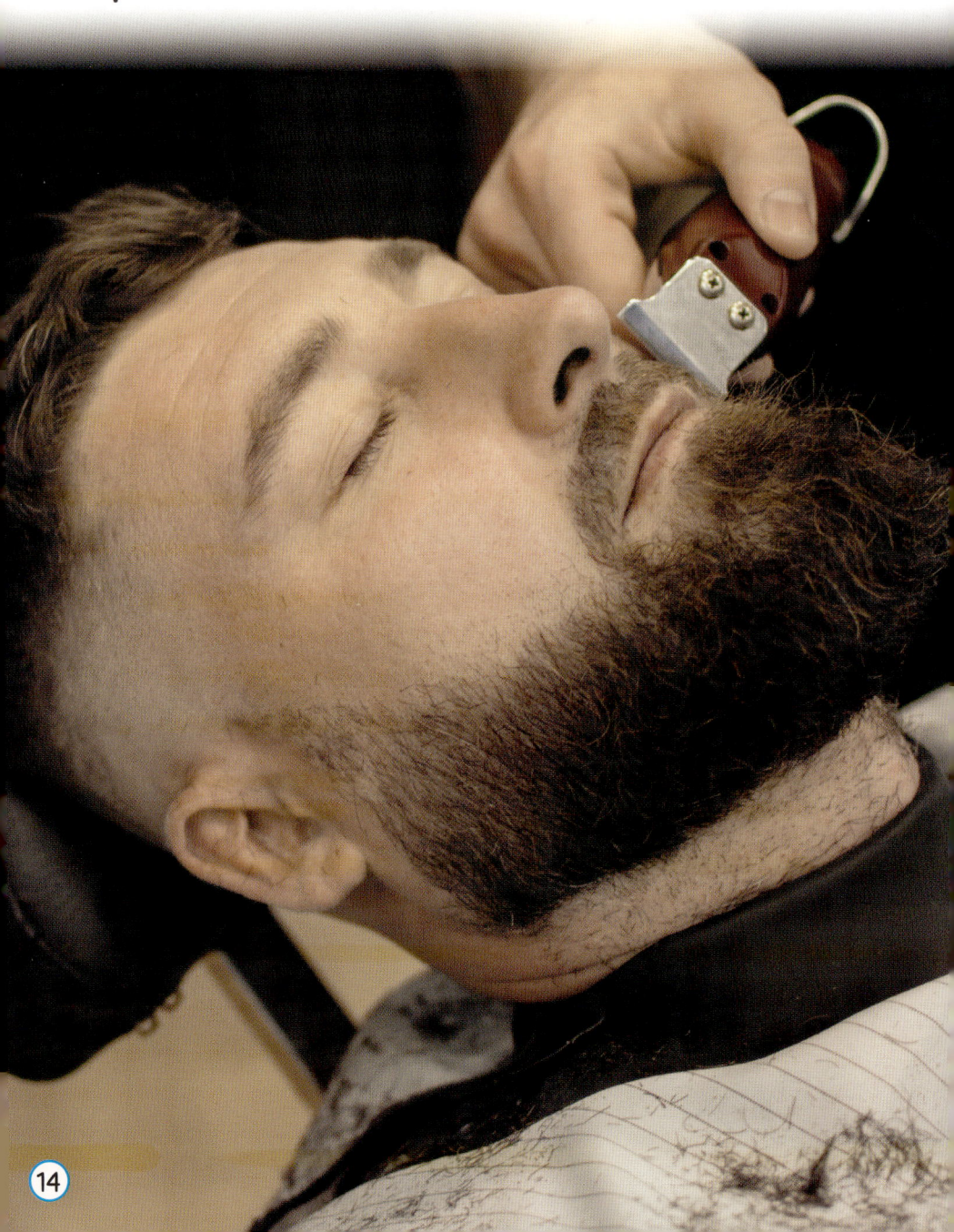

It can feel good to get a haircut. Now, he looks smart.

©2023 **BookLife Publishing Ltd.**
King's Lynn, Norfolk, PE30 4LS, UK

ISBN 978-1-80505-051-3

All rights reserved. Printed in China.
A catalogue record for this book
is available from the British Library.

Haircuts
Written by Charis Mather
Designed by Lucy Otter

An Introduction to BookLife Readers...

Our Readers have been specifically created in line with the London Institute of Education's approach to book banding and are phonetically decodable and ordered to support each phase of Letters and Sounds.

Each book has been created to provide the best possible reading and learning experience. Our aim is to share our love of books with children, providing both emerging readers and prolific page-turners with beautiful books that are guaranteed to provoke interest and learning, regardless of ability.

BOOK BAND GRADED using the Institute of Education's approach to levelling.

PHONETICALLY DECODABLE supporting each phase of Letters and Sounds.

EXERCISES AND QUESTIONS to offer reinforcement and to ascertain comprehension.

CLEAR DESIGN to inspire and provoke engagement, providing the reader with clear visual representations of each non-fiction topic.

AUTHOR INSIGHT:
CHARIS MATHER

Charis Mather is a children's author at BookLife Publishing who has a love for reading and writing. Her studies in linguistics and experiences working with young readers have given her a knack for writing material that suits a range of ages and skill levels. Charis is passionate about producing books that emphasise the fun in reading and is convinced that no matter how much you already know, there is always something new to learn.

This book focuses on /ear/ and /air/ and is a Blue level 4 book band.

Image Credits Images are courtesy of Shutterstock.com. With thanks to Getty Images, Thinkstock Photo and iStockphoto. Cover - bessyana, Little_Monster_2070, Pair Srinrat, Tonographer. 4–5 – BearFotos, Pixel-Shot. 6–7 – Africa Studio, Maliutina Anna. 8–9 – Aksinia Prokhorova, SFROLOV. 10–11 – a35mmporhora, Alex Vog. 12–13 – NikolaJankovic, Roman Samborskyi. 14–15 – FXQuadro, LDarko.